RUBBING TORSOS

RUBBING TORSOS
JOHN LATTA

 ITHACA HOUSE

Acknowledgement is gratefully made to the following periodicals where some of the poems in this book were first published: *Abraxas, Choice, Cincinnati Poetry Review, Epoch, Gegenschein Quarterly, Granite, Green House,* and *Terraplane.*

Cover design by Pierre Quichy

ITHACA HOUSE
108 North Plain St.
Ithaca, New York 14850

Ithaca House books are distributed by:
SBD
1606 Ocean View Ave.
Kensington, CA 94707

Library of Congress Cataloging in Publication Data

Latta, John.
     Rubbing torsos.

          I. Title.
PS3562.A77R8   811'.5'4   79-465
ISBN 0-87886-101-7

for Meropi Ypsilantis

There is no such thing as chance. A door may happen to fall shut, but this is not by chance. It is a conscious experience of the door, the door, the door, the door.

—Kurt Schwitters

CONTENTS

I

II

III

I

3 SEPTEMBER FOURTEENTH

The rain smirks, a quiet skirmish.
Land knits its brows,
making ruts.
Grinning like soap,
I spud through a washout.
Nothing is keeping me here, on the bridge
umbrellas bob like Cossacks
faking a genteel stomp.

Sometimes it's the humidity,
manhole covers
six feet off the streets.
Today it's something different.
You no longer carry me about like a burr,
I've dropped off
into this new earth.
Everything lopes by, terrific and easy.
There's no danger—
in this country, we drink the enemy
like beer.

When he spoke of her long, elegant nose,
it was a *proboscis*.

There were beetles under her eyelids:
Coleoptera, shiny-backed, green and fragile.
Her breasts were anthills, the nipples
for entrance and exit.
Lips were as soft as the *larvae* of *Lepidoptera*.
Lying on her back, she was helpless:
she moved her arms and legs
as if she were collecting the air.

When she spoke, pale, dappled moths
entered the air and flying
towards the lightbulb, caught fire

before proper identification.

Cyst, protuberance, palinode, morphology. . .
The first cautious fuck
In the big yellow room with plants, Botticelli,
Light shivers of doubt. A large loud
Fly coursing in skewed zeros.

Globular beads of
Sweat—dark, still, impervious, like
Fungi, like pitchblende, luminously
Alert, like plums, like berries, like
Beriberi, like pellagra, like algebraic

Formulas. Thinking of everything—
What a body is, how I debunked the bed—
I lowered a long rope ladder out
The only window saying with a deep breath & rather
Funnily "I feel like Venus

With a penis!" &
Missing the first rung,
Fell into an ornery space
Like a sprinter losing the first race &
Grinning in chagrin, she-wolf, my sidewinder.

Nerves bicker and shove each other
like the lights
of a marquee. A movie

starring James Dean
and plugged full of Japanese subtitles.
You're in it too—skin so continuous

and wealthy, a conveyor belt
for Grade A eggs. Cock is a thorn—
the northern shrike hangs

dead field mice on it like
Christmas ornaments.
Sweat is blunt, a minnow.

Unbuttoning one's clothes each night
is a way of speaking: *This is
home, kiddo, home.*

A stunning cunt! Crisp
lettuce! Fists roll into themselves
like sowbugs.

Girls no longer a fossil fuel.
Hoi polloi is no longer polite for Oh boy!
Smoking isn't inertia,
picnicking, algebra, or quick sex.
The planet isn't a surreal fish
or a pinched nerve.
How droll its orbit,
pouty like a question mark.
I wear entropy like an eyepatch,
this poem a telescope.
Saturn resembles a deviled egg!
I don't love you.

Or she's nice,
a beauty sponsored by the ice pick industry.
Metal is so keen,
its molecules follow like syllogisms:
    A. She's not a tuning fork against obesity.
    B. She's not another rank fidelity we wail against.
    C. She's not a skeptical achoo.
∴ D. This poem is called "From the One
       Who Never Made It
       Past the Grandstand of Your Heart."

8 COMING BACK TO A SNOWFALL AND A LETTER SAYING IT IS OVER, I WALK ALL NIGHT WHERE THERE ARE NO ROADS

The solid night
surreal like the snowplow
grinding out the fat dark. Out here
the loose ends of sympathy unravel
and burn a pointed blue spur. Cupping
my hands against the cold wind, or
high overhead my arms
winging a slow beat south.
The Greyhound back through Pennsylvania
like a bullet, a cluster bomb.
The terminal, stuffy travelers
lodged in the walls like shrapnel, or
arching out over these bare white hills,
hitting a dull sluff,
soft burial.

And days before, the rain big
like stray hairs, the sifting wind,
the near dry land.
Forget it, forget everything:
You call it ice, it's only bruised snow.

9 YOU'D HAVE TO BE CRAZY TO SAY IT WAS WORTH IT

for Jean Wu

There's something about us now that's like
Judy Garland singing "Somewhere over the
                                    Rimbaud. . .''
We've twisted like old, piled cars

or the witch's feet
after that big Kansan house felled her.
This isn't cocky half-French

belles lettres or drugs that make you famous
till you have to take drugs. This
is the tough new argument against sobbing.

The season is hellish here: even
parking meters sidle by snickering obscenities.
Jogging is the only company—I think of poor Toto

humming like a pocketbook under your arm.
Face it, wizardry isn't a drunken bout against
bigger fuckups, it's this lying.

Our angst strums a new lick, wavelengths
of hope like the rope a rock climber
pulls more numb. Ripstop dreamings of nylon,

particle cytokinesis like a shroff
of good fortune, any fissure so discreet
time doesn't matter. Tempo is

the verbena piercing my friend buffalo.
The land runs out and back with the railroads,
the Amish get stationwagons, astonishing!

Success isn't hitting rock bottom
and paydirt filling our mouths like gypsum,
or opening a geode: a seedling caught

in its teeth. O troubleshooter! O coup d'état!
Rearranging our histories isn't without Dolor-
the-body-bomb. But love isn't a cairn

we pile like hemorrhoids, plain turds—
what about overcrowding! Already we bite nails,
share visions, ailments, beds.

Her flannel shirt blouses neatly to conceal her
smallish & magnificent breasts
and I am looking & she knows it.

I long to say something so quietly **to her**
we would collapse
this too bountiful moment &

hush into an **interring traffic** of noiseless
yearning—two simple spoons resting
side by side on a blue-checked linen **cloth**

or two leaves, imperfectly green & **curling,**
complimenting the red of a recently-picked apple.
Two nights back I shook in my sleeves

like a boy alcoholic trying
to tell her what the woods were when,
young & angelic, I marched there

with my pine bough broadsword
protecting the silent furry ones. I, unseen,
and the Other, unseen, still

do battle in the cunning woods but
tonight her plaintive shiver is smiling way off
like a boathouse light &

my hand's barge shoves off, making
this, our mutual space, an invading &
spooky river.

Everything a tint this morning &
I refuse to sleep because
approaching is summer's funny chameleon

precursor, feminine, preterite & unchosen
like you in the thinking of whom my heart clenches
and sputters like a Browning Automatic Rifle

fired from the hip barring
any sentiment & lucratively mowing down
our own human species in some

banal & dirty war, cold & Korean.
So I deny my heart, my gun, my rallying cues
and enthuse myself with a crow

sawing yawnily in a stark tree.
I trust nothing but, hugging &
waylaying everything, my

body trembles like a leaf, aspen &
quaking, my desire unfolds one wan petal,
and so, often pauses.

I demand nothing.
I am awake all night.
I tread gently the growing traffic noises,

pooling like water. In the field
behind the granary I call out my sad
and stolid hope: *I love you*

with no reason & immediately feel
primitive as a leek.
This isn't everything. There's my

death, precise, reaching
out its claws, yearning & concealed—
black on black—

and sleep will never reveal what you do,
cut loose, caustic & raiding.

Between the furl of a wave's
Engulfing itself &
                    The dally of
A red leaf
Spinning off a tree

Is this
Simple sheen of
Quiet yellow light

Pressing damp hair
To damp hair

Everything's plain here

How I become cumbersome
With intention
How I drink late into the night
Nervous &
                    Clogged with
Stamina's own sweet boredom

Now
Tired of this bleating stoicism
Grinning away the dull ache
Tired of my heart
                    Sealed off &
Wrapped in spun wire

Tired of this feverish culling
Of Nature's too few
Startling indices

                    The siskin
In the pine
Tired of fear & its
Plodding dead foot
                    Tired of
The span my hand makes
Reaching out

I love you

Two plums ripening in a dark room
Or two clouds making galactic noise —any duality beyond
A mere numeral contrapuntal, any complaint
Of this universe.

Plumping a pillow in the morning "disheveling the
                                          dream mold"
Cold today with a troublesome hint of sparse rain

A city of doubt
A man so like a century of aphorisms
                    "O naughty reasoning reason" or
"A man thinks, a man is
Caustic soda dissolving the phenomenal smear into
Volatile quantae called Language"

Or "Vision is collision" so suddenly we veer off into
The personal

The way a match striking out into fire knows
A brief clarity akin to
A jazz combo's slipping avoidance
Of a fullblown melody line
                          the line coiling out of
                          a mess of sound

An apple paring on a white tabletop

Two lovers in mufti dancing
To the whirr of atomic orbiting
A plumb bob a wheel turning so quickly
It stills into fiction
                    a kind of adamant limbo
                    like a leonine yawn

Anything so blondely affecting

This year
Curling back on itself like a leaf in
Summer heat—we're settling in
Old & older

There's a ruthless beauty here we cannot name
The Good The Perfect
          "some particular of divinity"
Rendering tacit
All motion
A cigarette halfway to a mouth

How bothersome & omnivorous it is

Time snapping & pausing
An archer nocking a new arrow
A straw bale a clump of earth a cornice a wood rasp
                                        a radio
. Weighing all objects
With uncertainty asking again the maudlin questions
Is there enough time
                    what's next what's needed
Where is the hammer
Is the train here
What's the meaning of "umbrageous" is the day
Over so soon

What's French for "guttersnipe" why is it raining
Is it raining
Is there something pernicious like a nematode "in
                                        our blood"
Is this the lingering ache

Is our seed collection intact
The sycamore balls all spiny like
Black sea urchins
Maple wings

The dull coins of elm & our
All too fruitless anatomies
Swishing side by side in fortuitous & easy clothes
    I take a sprig of a leap
    I would rather be a sheep
O what subtle appraisal of delight
                    what a shimmering instant
To hold
A single bold inkling of
Something beyond

This stirring broth of listless days
Ah the stamina then
To paraphrase with a shout "O dear

Here's something"

                ❦

Oh I am a ridiculous man this table is so small &
Today I am so big benign nearly popely

O love love love
Is this "failingly compelling" or "compellingly
                        failing"
Adverbs poke poke poke
Why no gratuitous stability stability stability
Why such sweaty arpeggios

                    "what sort of ponderousness"
In no respite in reprise
Here here here how insupportably clamorous I become

Language isn't so strong befittingly
The sun is "niggardly" or "prudent" today
A stray beam is nipping a rooftop
I am reeling in terrific havoc
                              shooing Destiny
Gregarious like a child
Putting an index finger in its puggish nose

Days shuttle by with a taut precision
A bonesetting
Sheer & cherubic simultaneously coffee & Gauloises
Boiling water in a simple

Kettle ah the
Utensils of a normal life a tugboat nosing a freighter
Boy o boy two tons of almond oil the
Bliss of it rotates me into a *rôtisserie* where pensively
Yellowing a whole pig is grinning "doggedly"

What happenstance is there in such a trance

Knocking about like a cowboy in Paris
A woman with an umbrella stooping in a gutter
                              "what a man's day
Toots" I quip bracingly she begins railing like a
                              gallinule "so
Here's a zebra finch thinking of pinching my lunch"
Elephantinely spunky she is
Rather rank and o what contagion

20

I cough into my red bandanna and it's suddenly
Night and I am relentlessly
Envious of what the sun is seeing

Yawping like a big saxaphone over the North
American continent
In its summer outfit
Hearsay is always so annoyingly courteous & we're

So necessary & adroitly
Happy with a stubborn grace
Like the kinetic lope of guy lines over a pulley
Being so perpetually

In and out of love in this "souvenir" century that
"dasn't" mean memorable

II

II

Our animal sensibilities have grown
hard through fear and ceaseless myopia.
On the telephone, your voice is acrid
like a lizard stiffened by formaldehyde.
Your words smell of science. As if,
stretched and pinned to beeswax,
you had become weak-bladdered,
corpulent, and morose.
You cannot talk now. I become conscious
of the noise of the splitting of your skin.
Like the even humming of a long wire
that sags under the weight of lies and ice
along a hard-packed road out of here.

There is a polar
emptiness about me now.
I am not a bear, yet

I shuffle through these streets
as though drugged by asphalt.
I fetch your letters

from a soft cubicle.
It is not unlike an open mouth.
The day is a casual fixture:

a 60 watt Edison in the public library.
Even my feet seem superficial.
One day last summer, after fucking

on the dunes near Frankfort,
I shook you like a shoe,
gently tapping your head against the lake,

leaning you facedown as sand
sifted from your mouth in a pile.
You did the same for me.

We wore each other as comfortably
as Oxfords
for the rest of the day.

Everywhere is a smattering of lament.
Incisions of bleeding doubt.
Tired of waiting bruises me like a doormat.
These scuffle marks hang on my skin
like oranges, only plummeting off
if I leave quickly, trailing
the Cessna like a sash.
Flight defined as a shadow's wreckage,
the perfect cleavage of feet and ground.
Resignation a part of my anatomy,
a razor blade gone loco
and no loss of blood.
It doesn't matter anymore,
It doesn't matter anymore
ho hums like an electric drill,
the shrillness that occupies wooden hearts
released like a tough dirge.
And the walls of these houses, upright
with unknowing neglect, straight
like the path a sigh travels
as it leaves the body. It is leaving now.

There. An Americanism of mosts!
Here only these words
like tracings of abandoned episodes:
symbiosis, schism, rat's hide,
nauseous, vetch, pointillism, continue.
Still friends jolts hard like coffee,
Ann Arbor, the snow, and wanting
to throw you hard akimbo like a sled,
jump on with a viciousness
even the French have never seen.

A deft sodality! Cigarettes or
long hair and a tent. Hitchhiking
across northern Michigan,
I lied to everybody and they liked it.
In Mesick, crude puns sheltered me
like a disease: *I'm sick in Mesick,
ha ha*, stranded so long
in that pothole of a town.
A dipshit mystic assailed me
like a cruddy stench for two hours
under a Standard gas sign.
He had a dishonorable discharge
for meeting Jesus in Germany
and did oil paintings of moose
with antlers like celery stalks.
"For one thing, as a kid
I jacked off one hell of a lot—"
is how he explained it.
There was a girl
he would have crossed ten continents for.
He told me to wait for that kind
of girl. Another half-assed joke
pierced me like a fuchsia:
I'm not that continent.
Some wiseguy had yelled "Do it again —"
when I kissed you where you let me out.
I gave him the finger.
Later in the gas station he said
"You were goin' real good, why'd y'stop?"

and told me about one of the guys
in the café across the street
that had a pacemaker in his heart.
"It did him real good
to see a thing like that."

The Y on Wabash and 8th
is full of gawky signs like hookers,
cursory fuckups, small lacunas
of satisfaction carved out
of the day: *No Smoking in Bed.*
It's a backlash
from the Great Chicago Fire.
Up here on the 13th floor,
trolleys below zipping by
like a string of briefcases and yawns,
big boats on the snotty lake
churling like overstuffed rats.
It's the 30th of July.

A spunky day for art! Pissarro!
Toulouse-Lautrec! dashing
to an all-night pizzeria
and back for Picasso! Hot nights,
walking too near the frumpy Buckingham
fountain, getting soaked,
trammeled like glue sniffers by
those flashy lights that wipe the air
like airport beams. Later,
groping beneath some Grant Park
trees, hectic and uneasy about dogshit
and muggers, like so many other
thousands of everyday couples,
plying our newfound rarity.

The old Plymouth is out
back, one rear wheel jacked up
like a dog letting water.
High schoolers stripped it—
the parts for old Buicks
and Chevies now called Mabel,
Oglestern's Tirewhacker,
Mother Bertha, or The Bullet.

Beyond is the cornfield
like an airstrip of corduroy
that pulls the house, the silos,
the barns, and the new Ford pickup
toward the fisted watertower
in Peugeot, Iowa.
Here the sheriff's deputies
cruise US 20 like empty windsocks,
volunteer firemen pitch horseshoes
into pockmarks that pacify
the land's flatness.
Truck drivers leaving
Chicago notice a change in women.

This air is ability. Like
an Olympic swimmer, it's been
crackling pro-Simian

all week. Down here is fog
the palms sling low
on hips mornings and gun

through like dinghies by night.
Egrets and sandhill cranes
lift by the road's edge

and settle like litter after
we pass. Overhead,
the sun is a barge

slogged across the sky
by some wheedling, unseen tug.
It is paint, or beer

overflowing. Noon
turns conversations fat
inside these squat white

houses that sweat
like urinals. Everything
outside ourselves

hammers: these bodies
become scrap metal,
the beach an anvil. This greed

for tan is like that for
good pork. We will sport it
like cynicism or new shoes.

Scraping north,
the car radio knots back into itself
like windblown hair.
Quiets beneath overpasses.
Old snow peeks up out of a field
like the sheet of an untucked bed.
The road map clutches my knees,
wet clothing, a tablecloth.
It is all easy to accept:
the miles and miles wound in like kite string,
nothing how we left it.
Time doesen't matter, it noses
through cabbages and sheep sorrel, a sour pig
trying to uproot us. Friends die
snorkeling—fuck tragedy.
Sending out runners
like a beseiged Greek city,
talking about old girlfriends,
we're too lucky,
suicidal and just.
Behind the stuffy, underfed Datsun,
a thin sticky substance coats the highway.
A snail's soft underpinnings.

I become hostile with every new
Reckoning & long
To hoove a dry riverbed
South
The night air beseiged by
Desire & watering holes evenly
Spaced out like
Little little little spittle
Gobs a farmer finds
Hoeing the bean row

Today I repaired a chair before
Repairing to my friend The Criminal's lair
Where we whittled
Anxiety down
To a sweet sodden melody

I plodded about sullenly
Replacing fresh linen with handfuls
Of chive & my friend
Poured over *The Journal of Chilly Nights*

"The Gang got jumpy attending
A certain surly obsequy
My horse therein dropped into
A ravine
As I moribundly
Sought a place
To pee & shaking it off
I spoke the cowboy's
One word *Lonesome*
As a horny toad slammed into

A rock shaped like
A tornado thus ending —"

Everything is beckoning & a sibilance
In the long grasses
Brushes my dog's hair
To a ruff
A standing oily scarf of fear
I call Dog
My fingers begin to drop
Off

One is a bullet
One is a burr
One is a sausage
One lopes off into the woods
Tail between its legs
One bursts into several nodules
One joins the thumb making a saguaro cactus
One is a little oinker
Nosing the
Teats of a big sow
One sulks in a corral
Two white horses whinny about it

Here in the West
Every code becomes a coda

"So one night
Lying awake between
My fire & my dog
In a treeless open

A single tree
Will bundle and thrust us
Up to the sky's blue limit of sway &

I will know
To cut myself
Notch & saw
To thump the earth & be stilled by it—"

III

III

1

Night, the truculent buzz saw, the leonine helicopter of ash, light
inside houses smiling like a new lover. An armchair basks like a
                                                          giant
panda, lint beneath the radiator goes frowsy with acceptance. A bed
wobbles, a mother's buckling indignity toward unshaven armpits
                                                    —it grinds,
gnashing its teeth. Our annulment of the canaries continues: astride
a pocketful of cannibals, called a decoy, choosing you from the
                                                        aviaries
of radish parchment—there are rivets like sleeves of light sweeping
me together in a mound. This mud is called the Strand by several
                                                        species
of butterflies, names emblazoned in sleazy, yellow fervor—tiger
swallowtail, red admiral. Rub your nose in it, use it as an
                                                    aftershave
called Stamina. Correct me if I am wrong.
          This is a letter of pins, a treetop in a mailbox
christened Fertility like the sudden overtures of an electrical switch
to a postage meter. It will take you anywhere. In a locomotive
fashion, ladies wear trains, this poem is called "Veiling the Tracks
the Metaphor Travels Over." I match my breathing to yours, dogs
speaking in pleasant and reasonable monotones, livestock outside
wilting like strippers' tits.

2

A hard penis, a tennis racket, a trellis, a visionary gradient, radial
symmetry, Goodyear's, a blimp, a shrieking pimple, a zeppelin
                                                        posing
for a hamburger, a trenchcoat igniting, hoof and mouth disease,
                                                          Louis
Pasteur, pastoral side effects, an appendectomy, an insect gall, a

wormy navel, ending the novel, beginning the novel, *Ralph*
                                        Fredericks
had a printed-page hardon, a papal pardon, a nuisance, a modular tic,
a nuance, Fred Astaire, Ginger Baker, *The Jazz Singer*, *les flics*,
le cinéma, an enema, a douche, saran wrap, sticky ice, seducing
                                        the
typewriter, Rh negative, a thoroughbred matrix, a steeplechase,
                                        an
escaping church. It's April and agnostic! A cunning cunnilingual
affability! Political candidate! Imbecimile! Horseshit! A sequel
                                        of
puns, an ordinary run, a dashing stomach ache, a fart, a fault,
an earthquake, a diamond cutter, ice rink, ringworm, a fur-
                                        loughed
wench, a wurzy finch, potatoes degroined without liability,
                                        cardinal
wantonessness, fear, worth whrrrs, trunneled wisteria, hysteria
sprinting through an underbrush of slobs, a glacial molaine, arcs
like glands, arrows ridding whalestems under tundered absolvancies
of treacled soap, fish treadfare voltive, seriffing tangible sauce,
rall strubel, megaphone sumstra, a morphic cyst, tremelos of wust,
"fiction," "troughs," "sloe," "trusk," "ear," "clemency."

3

Morning dissipates itself like a clogged nose, straddles the cheesy
underbelly of night, fornicates with the automobile exhaust that
slithers like a salamander off the pavement. We remember a dead
goldfish with fondue, a horned toad in the backyard and begin
                                        to shutter
the windows against the foliage of some insouciant shrubbery.
                                        "Dear
sibling weather, We shrug like palsied shepherds and notice only
a tinny pang of our former immobility. The clouds are peeling
                                        like
old paint. The flattering irony is this: I never thought I would

be writing you, but Oh fugging insomnia, and it's happening to me!
Sign me, No Longer Frigid in St. Louis'' The trolley licks the
                                                            profligate
spoon that feeds it, we sketch intimate subways on legal pads,
rubbing our torsos in the feverish light. Oh pristine lethargy! Oh
sweltering cacaphony! The catatonic typewriter, the tacit monkey,
the thumb meeting the forefinger in the invention of lust! Foreign
languages, two quid, a tip on the desk, a note slicing the field of
                                                            air
beneath the door—*"Mon cher garçon aux longues jambes, À la
                                            piscine. . .*
le baiser français. . .vachement!" Oh the fleeting anaerobic comforts!
No more atrophic passions, no more aphasiac scoldings, no more
                                                            new
footballs—we're replacing the replacing the
                            A pickled hill in a jar,
a rubber egg, a doorknob, a hall of buried insolence and gregarious
damp we sink our elbows into, a map that measures the frequency
of bone marrow. A blacksmith is pounding out the petals of a
                                                            tepid
rose. Another man is fixing a foreign car. He is using a toothbrush
and he is scowling. Someone else's nose is bleeding chewing gum.
                                                            It is
so hot all the tables and chairs have wilted and lie stranded about
like deflated balloons or ships in the doldrums. Every so often
one scitters away like a crayfish or quivers like something big dying.
Lying here separate and still, delusion a useless magnifying
glass. Look here, lean together like a teepee, name your parts
after the furniture. Arms, legs, back, mattress.

4

The bland tension of the afternoon is alarming, it rusts like an ulcer,
a new fender dinged by torpor. The sky is planning a new astrin-
                                                            gency,

never forget the possibility of siege. Be ubiquitous like the creek
chub, the chubby creek, chess, a racehorse spiked with lan-
                                                    thanum. Here
the rain scrambles down like a marsupial and I miss everybody's
birthday. "In 1924, Josie Salerno started a walk across a field. She
had just turned eighteen and had college plans.The field was being
renovated to become the North American Museum of Living
                                                    History.
Josie became a part of the display and continued to walk across
                                                    the field.
Visitors to the museum only noticed that her hair turned whiter
                                                    and whiter."
Teenagers flit by packed in cars like sardines, Sardinian
faggots. Everything is fun while it lasts—the firebombing of
                                                    a lambchop,
heading like a zero into New Jersey, that deaf mute mimicking
                                                    himself
by saying nothing, the way art is today. "Some thought it was
                                                    the snow
that had been made to fall permanently inside that part of
the museum. However, the snow was turned off nights and
                                                    museum
officials knew Josie was getting older. *Let her retire*, the director
decided, *we'll just have to advertise for a replacement.* Josie
had a birthday party right there in the museum." Oh senti-
                                                    mental
turgidity, not quite beachy, frenetic enough in dungarees and
                                                    sneakers,
combing combing the bald waves. Red rover, red rover, send
England right over — skittish gulls spank off, we push planks into
the tide loaded with the hours of our wilt. The blessings. Our feet
turn to salt, we can't get enough of it.

    Sneaker's Crossings, R.I. (AP) — Museum officials of the
North American Museum of Living History today reported
a new display entitled "The Birthday Party." Visitors are
invited to enjoy cake and ice cream during regular museum
hours.

Back, a ministerial bloom of selfsame limpidity and turning
effluence in the air, our car spokes up out of this oil emulsion
like an island, a pod of disfigured hope. The size of an earlobe.
                                                    A fat
kid's navel you noticed on the waterfront at summer camp. The
                                                    lifeguard
is explaining the buddy system. The hands clasp to splice
the arms. Surface diving, the air is something sweet bursting on
                                                    your
tongue. Your ears hurt. We pack ourselves in—salvation like
                                                    this
is a pen with refillable cartridges. The only difference between
                                                    meaning
and contempt is this limp sandpiper on a blue platter called
Futility. It isn't ours.

                              5

Culling brio, the quick pulp of a primrose, the wind comes down
like a famished noose. Pursed lips. This is dusk lassoing the
                                                    trees,
pulling taut, a pony tail, a node trammeling this end of the
                                                    earth.
This is a dog show, even the lichens line up like pedigrees. No
                                                    more
tail wagging. I troop out the ribbons like lingerie, hanging out
these husks of a stiffened lethargy, ovaries. This is autumn,
a menstrual period, a sexual flush—the same dopey nostalgia is
                                                    kicking
through the leaves, the inner linings of the uterus. And nothing
is new—peevish October, bilious like evaporated milk,
Vietnam, our impotency attaching *this* to a grenade for the
                                                    lieutenant,
our poverty like a cesarian scar, our boisterous unconcern, a Fiat
humming empty near a courthouse, our monuments like
extinguished afterthoughts, our misplaced feelings, our secrecy,
everything like a fart in a crowded room.

6

Night again. The planet and I: still so uneasy about
                                        each other. I wear
waders, cheesecloth, and shoulder pads—I have
                                                learned
what she likes.
                        Oh lackadaisical spindrift! The stars
into everything again, what a mess! This target,
                                    that vortex
like an anteater's snout, a quill, several quills, Orion's
belt, a prolixity of formulas in the wake of the
                                    soporific field.
A hovercraft is plaat-plaating into winter again like
                                            industrial
spontaneity, I am Rebuff, my fire is a table of second-
                                                    rate
wines. New frost brillos the clipped lawns, "tomor-
                            row we will dissect
a beakerful of leg cramps." Camping is the new
                                    currency,
we pack our money in jars like aspirin and tell lies
                                    to keep warm.
Our hands turn to molluscs, we swap boxes of un-
                                        opened
hunger for hooks and a common play in football.
                                    Number 48
ties a fly on the 9 yard line, saving the game, the big
                                        game,
"a safari and gin, thanks." Somewhere a rhino is
                                    panhandling
through Nebraska.

is extraordinary like housewifery:
a pin is dough-on-the-Styx, a wiener roaster
for a biddy Rabelais. Contraceptive

foam: the resin of knotty pine, coniferous foreplay:
this is why voodoo is money, a seamstress in 1894
embroidering a hoop of skin: everything

so catholic: ice cream, neapolitan waterlooed
out of Russia like a boy making jerkwater. It
tenses like diuresis, two beers

and the testicles purr in sockets.
A tomcat sipping *vermin bianco* through a straw.
A rolling pin is pig-in-a-plankton net: our net

concern consternated and shoved away
the table: read "cock" or "count " It comes
off the tongue like "vin *au lit*re," how lucky

the metric system is, dousing the bed, witch
hazel spronnng, a before and after photograph
of Kitty Genovese. The sleeping

resembles a word like "onyx,"
or "oyster." A barnacle, a ptarmigan in a snowbank,
a family reunion, sheets like gills.

"In the paramecium, the pulse of the contractile
                                        vacuole
moves water in amounts proportionate to its
                                        salinity."
Breathing is wonderful: so Jurassic,

Mexican, electricity reeling through whole cells
like a love affair, shirtless, contagious.
A yawn comes like a neurosis: a slender movement.

The hug, the body's jump rope. In the sink's
sallow dishwater "my hands *sud* south," daphnia
and chloe, two tongues, twin kites

hitting the earth: the dry banks of a river caking off.
A pinup girl is shedding pounds like a welterweight,
the last axe Abe Lincoln ever swung: dreamy,

ain't it. Here comes Hamlet with chef's hat
and barbecue fork, something stinks of kerosene:
a Corinth lamp, lambasting the meat, a rocket
                                        applying

for citizenship. A packaged cow in a supermarket,
idling an eraser, teething ring, cud.
Sangria, tequila, flotilla, lentil soup,

"Attila the hone" scouring pads. The knife
is what the bridge never called
"tree." That is fork talk: how the foresters

call it "controlled burn," what is salience?
Marilyn Monroe: I want a mournful sandwich:
I look up the lichen on her slopes—

fern family. "Well, it's not a gymnosperm,"
says Pogwald the possum, "we ain't got no
                                        trampoline."
Quonset huts scuttle by like small

gamin: the first day of hunting season.
Harry's cessna with airplanes
hit the delta like sonic boom: shook her pans.

Sylvia wept Ooooooo oooooooo ooooooo
A piece of rock with an Army haircut
followed Liz like beer chasing bourbon.

Two feet flapping like sequins
into the lolling dark: a lupus loping through lupine:
sinuous and bode: suburbia.

A rabbit out of a thicket: a jar breaking:
clapping after everyone has stopped.
Our hero's batting slump: "The first kiss

like gum making terrain under a school desk."
A finger pulled out: cinnamon, sticky, whose mouth?
Cock is kickstand, kamikaze, isthmus: this fire

burns and insulates the wood: only voices fill us
and fill in for us: Lesley gores the relish, Judy
garlands with garnish and everybody sups.

Two shepherds and I downing bacardi is
something like the Spanish Armada's medical chart.
Or Wall Street plummets
to zero and they call it a pin stripe:
history just can't be another
lump in the throat.

The day eddies on like a gourmet, we smoke
the cheerless bouncer.
Turn in empties.
Our stomachs drip excitingly,
their homing pigeons honing in
to the brain with memos:

"Bake a single calamity,
loop a beach about your head
like a turban.
Talk pork.
Stay in bed all day."

Two shepherds.
Voices like magma, 16 rpm.
Sheep bleatings pulled out of the air
like the hard words
before a fistfight.

A porcupine, the field hunches up.
Winter bellies in
for the kill.
Here only carcass keeps.
Like historical markers,
blood clottings have it in for us.
Our past throttles shut.
Behind us the wake of a motorboat,
waves curled like cauliflower,
a ram's head.

Everything freezes.
Whole circulatory systems
step out of our bodies,
crimp about
testing the planet:
arthropoda, arachnid, sheepish, ouch. . .

Connect electrodes to the trees.
The only mosquito is
inside our tent called Electrocardiograph.
Its dying is soufflé
failing. Nothing works right!
The air is a magnetic force field,
our nostrils flame up like iron filings.
Ears ring. Hair bustles
around static, a coonskin cap
like Davy Crockett! The slush
is salt, our muscles
shrug off their tethers, become trout
limp in these creel of arms,
Small birds collapse
like flat tires,
lounge with binoculars, bikinilike,
on branches. *Nouveaux*
riches fungi.
An algal bloom—each cell paunches.
Becomes a succulent, shovels out
sodium like a fireman.
Stores water for years!
If we could only lift our arms,
the billy clubs banging
useless against our sides, pick
this old scab off,
or fling back winter like a fish
too small for the frypan.

is not a rhinoplast.
is an aureole, new Volkswagen
beating a lick around a track:
gnomish Chomskian burnout,
hitting the wall.
is gum stretched over a new tooth:
needs no teething ring,
maenad pacifier.
is a ghost limb.
Its absence is rubbed and exciting.

You're a man and this shouldn't matter,
but you can't sleep nights.
Don't count sheep, don't count in
binomial cursories:
just drive hard
and count on the checkered flag
waving you on in.

PASTORALE BAKED ALASKA

The literary Aleutians.

I strike a match like striking a profile
of Egyptian furniture.
Tetrahedral tits in a dry landscape.
A cow burns like a Christmas pitch pine,
each steak broiling and stoking:
simultaneous waxwing cantata.
A weathervane looks good
enough to eat: they spread neon
on it, call it a frankfurter,
rubber obelisk.
Three shepherds priming a new evolution:
Zippo lighter, solar
plexiglas, Brenda Starr nosethumb.
Fie, fie, fire, the center
of everything.
Here comes the adventure.
Here comes the adventure starring
Nick Acne and sidekick, Sebum.
"Peachums! Sorghum. It's Clint and Steal!"

Golly! what an appetite! moiling oceanery shenani-
                                          gans like
Righting a sailboat in nasty weather. You lease a
                                          roiling
Estuary of mope, me smoking so the heart stutters
Askance looking for a loophole lee: a loblolly pining
                                          because love is
Chancy and wondrous and bleats! Today its occasion
Is this blade of grass thumbing its little nose
Against the craft that pins it. Stepping out
Now arm in arm with a stitch meeting a
                                          parasolipsism...

Gee! A pollen air, quick! where's the dissecting
                                          index?
Or where's this glance lancing off a postcard sullenly
Eulogizing the Florida swayback
Kite and its nesting habits? O what is
Essential isn't this heliotropism, it's the continental
                                          self.

Knifing is so pedestrian: it's the sheathing makes a
                                                man
Agreeable and sear. Then sometimes just our shadows
                                            lengthen
Trying new deposits like the water striders coupling
Here: this pool a vestibule. O fucking calisthenics!
                        fuck the little polemics:
All art is arbitrary like "natural beauty" or this
Random credulity washing over you like a rum and
                                                coke
Intercontinental sailboat race. Here I am: mister
                democracy in a pressure cooker, a
Neo-Marxist love affair with a spatula and all the
                                        spuds you'll
Ever need soaking overnight in the kitchen stink.

Yes, our olympic hiking through Aristotelian ferns
Isn't so theatrical as my own centripetal force, dear.
                                        A javelin
Hanging in the air sponges the earth it finally cleaves.

Monocotyledonous, shimmering, our lives rakishly parallel like the
Insidious veins of this blade of grass we chew
Consolingly down to its white core. Sometimes our talking makes
the silence ache,
Hermetic and temporal like a pan of water boiling suddenly in a
new vacuum—
Air stumping out: a torso, cluster of limp lungs. A love affair
sagging, this succoring
Emptiness what can't be bought in a fire sale even if the house
didn't implode
Leveling in the heat: a lake of planks shuffling, cardlike, a
a beginning.

Sources of this weltschmerzing smarting aren't our roots, they're
now, this rivulet
Combining with another and another all named Today,
How boring and little and sweaty! Why not Lack of Sleep or
Schlep Over Here, Buster
When it's so trifling hard to even wallow in our own inertia like
menopausal elk. What we need is
An amino acid pausing to reconsider before the spark jumps
Revving. O a motorcycle kickstarting, o radial symmetry, o
double helix!
This isn't working. An RNA jeep won't buck
Zoology, only this life limping home from the door leading out
of its house.

Jeu d'esprit is necessary here—vernal and skew like this funky
                                        orbiting id we can't
Eke ourselves out of when love lumbers off: some leaves still
                                claiming the space a tree
Recently left. O where were we that day in the natural centro-
                        specificity of things asking what
Enigma meant and *zeugma*. . .there we were. Simpering like collies
                                        and quirky to
Meet women. Using drugs like books trying to level with that
                                old itch—the blood
Yearning for a target beyond the crosshairs that plug veins and
                                                arteries.

Cynicism's the dry rot I bore into like an insect making a gall of
                                        tough remorse
Ossifying a weltanschauung leaf by feverish leaf. It isn't
                        working: the placenta
Needles us in our dreams like an old lover wanting news: how
                this skin leaves so imperceptibly! What
We know now is delirious and camp and our moulting only whets
                                                a new
Animism. Someday our clothes will chorus out of bed mornings
                        without us, a sleeve will
Yawn over a drawer for a cigarette weaseling out of reach.
                A buttonhole sniffing doglike.

Chide & chide the snide jive! What's so
Handsome & unremitting & penetratingly up-the-nose about
                                                    being so
Rabidly stalwart & decorously alive like a bat so
Innocuously signed by Orlando Cepeda as to clobber & fun so
Subtly a sensibility of mere goof & we possibly behaving so?

How is it "twenty or so evening grosbeaks" or "what
Everyman is" is so multimedia-istically boring to what
Numismatists call "coining a phrase"? What
Kulchur we pound! So easy & arrayed! Like what
Evening is without a single bleary beer to anchor what
Lies preternaturally evident like the salient jut of so what.

Just this boy and this girl and The
Above beckoning like the smell of something sautéed and
Nourishing on a Sunday morning. I love the
Infinite and the indigo bunting and the snow bunting hit by a BB I
Cared for for a day and a night in northern Michigan.
Every boy is this same and sharply delineated

Exculpation of the gods and the angels and the ghosts and the
Lambent walk of the plain, happy dead fetters us all
And every girl allows it only with the intricate sexual diffidence
Inherent in any lore. Like love's lone lobo lopes dislodging loose
                                 loam:
Now we must live with such a language's dull lolling. Not
Exactly English, my hero confuses the words

Bailiff and *bâillement* and when the
Experts trot out notions of subliminal egoism,
Absolves to feint like a mothball, slugging the air with odor
Like practical science, down on hands and knees, practical and
                                scientific.

IV

The new age. A cloud is shaped like a cross
between a salami and a shoe. A sausage with laces
untied. Pigskin. Only Saturday is

this soft, a sluggard. I down chablis blanc
from a bottle. Football players knock about like
fat German pretzels. It is ridiculous: no-

body is ever hurt. I am trying to tackle a
cloud out of the sky using a telepathic
concentrate. Something like trying to piss,

bladder empty, a pigskin— only the brain
is quarterbacking. They call it cloud
destroying, its god isn't Siva. It's a

sieve. Liquid draining from a liquid
containing material: a thundershower begins.
—The chablis? No. —The game called? No.

—A Noh play? Maybe. This isn't fish-
in-buckets or cats and dogs. This is
pepperoni: the land doughs out, thick

on the edges like a smudge, a metaphysical
pizza. The teams peel off jerseys like
kimonos, they're getting drunk on pure Nirvana.

Slipshod, jejune, the days acquainted
with bedevilry: autumn's
three-pronged tail tailing off
over the hills in a haze. Death
is a decorative thing! St. George
knew this when he slew
the dragon: a shy conventional look
betrayed him, re-sheathing
the sword with a swagger. There's
little to explain. Today's weather
is curt, exclamatory but a woman
in a blue chemise shilly-shallies
pinning clothes to a clothesline
across the street. Sparrows
near the feeder disperse and
regroup blusteringly. Memory is
somewhat like this—*how appropriate,*
how inappropriate. Like
this acorn reminding me a little of
the 8-year-old Mozart performing—
capped, brow darkened with intent—
for the emperor's nephews.
They'd rather be kiting,
or running hoops with sticks
between the urn-shaped hedges.
The one that becomes a bulbous-nosed
courtier—but this is later of course! —in
a petty romance by a French gentleman
oft-besotted by chuckling women and
red-vested adjutants, is itching all over
and dares not scratch. Oh how is it

a discreet puckish songbird
can disgorge so fittingly
high in a red oak in October
just when the pharmacist's daughter
spies Wilson and Anne running
through the cornfield, holding hands?
How is it I can disjoin
so suddenly and go?
Soon—winter's too eager quiet
and the nights lit by
my stubbornness and nothing else.
In one dream I am a girl of the prairie
writing in her diary. "I will have
my simple wedding. I will be—for a short
while—perfectly content."

You arrive like General Custer, outlaw this gunslinger
and buckle some infidel pact
to my shoulder blades as if it were football Saturday.

It isn't and the helmet I am carrying is a fishbowl
full of stasis, a deliberate kitty of knots.
Here, strap it on. If you didn't jerk so, they

wouldn't call you Whiplash. Each morning
I set cream on your porch and some malingering tom-
cat
licks it clean as a new bayonet. A recruit's

thin smile. The sky is a fish belly up, love is
like this or that, the war isn't over. They'll never
design a commemorative stamp big enough to patch it

Only momentarily & then I am throwing my silly
mind's shadow on any other piece of
seemingly Taoist clutter.

For instance— one summer I kept a big sorrowful toad
beneath an overturned pail all summer &
galvanized thus all possibility of escape.

The woods called me so I dropped *The Girl
of the Limberlost* in a hedgehog's hole
and ran out-of-doors seeking material for a myth.

Chewing wintergreen leaves my mouth got fresh &
I kissed the first little bird I noticed.
No sparrow but a brown creeper—

all day I snuck up & down tree trunks
fibbing like a sapsucker in seersucker.
The next day my sister & I played ponies in the shy
                                                dusk

and my father frightened my mother with an elk's
head peeking around the side of the picture window.
The year memorized itself & I despaired in the wood-
                                                shed

over a dead field mouse where I never, in all
my ponderable skippiness, got tanned.

The dead toy gaily with us today
while in Greece hungry kids swipe oranges off
fruitstands & eat them crouching
behind three-wheeled carts. Snafus everywhere:
polyps of coral off the coast of Florida going white
in dying, exciting the regatta members sailing
over a permanent blue patina.

O I am thinking of the first time I thought
thoroughly & throughout though not through
any locale but my own third grade desk:
"I'm in love with the principal's daughter" &
I sent her the one embarrassing card in my 39 cent
                                        bundle—
the one that said "I love you"
and had two bright parrots beaking each other
on the same branch of the same tree.

Days later I noticed her slipping the card
out & examining it so closely death's
wind seemed to shiver me love's timbers &
I giggled aloud like a foreigner,
overly excited, saying over & over
"There is smorgasbord in America— it is good."
The next day I caught her
gaily kissing Johnny Burrows, the hoodlum, and

delighting in anger, broke all my old toys.

"Dear antithesis, the city tickles me pink—
my synapses nappy like a Negro's hair
on the corner of auburn and retina, lounging

a victorious tic. Ah, prehensile turnstiles! What
an atom-smashing day! Hello to Uncle Hunk,
bringing home a democratic mug: tell him I'm no
                                            dirty
socialite. O sweet! O plaintiff sesame! Life
is confusing: yesterday visiting
a courthouse in the Bronx, drunks

slobbering over *Loveletter versus
The State of New York.* Beating a steep path now:
the linen exchange isn't the stock exchange—

I know that. Carrying salvos of grief like
an extra pair of socks. Enter the septic tankard,
USS Weepy Beer, or the adoration of the tragi-

comedia delta artist. What a tart! You can't
love the missus tyrannosaurus any better than
the viscous petiole of the camellia.

Wha? This is St. Valentine's Day! The city
leaf says so by intrusion of its lobes:
foist, zecchino, turd. Love, Ferg."

Solitary angel, mugwump, Esau. . .
my forebears slumping over thick beers,
berating, large-lipped, the Scottish dank.
By claiming kin, I reclaim
a fathomable reticulate vernacular:
one loop of thread in the net
of family. Euchre or whist
with the uncles—the oily cards falling
with quiet slaps, the muffling
white expanse of cloth, George's
watery mirth. As if the table,
circular, and us four, lobar,
seated to circumferentiate perfectly
this, our common axial space,
were some somber and pale ocean form, hardly
animal or plant, but nodding
and bobbing, collusive and frayed,
miles deep in this, the most generous deep.
My father asks "What's trump?" and
George heaves the joke about spades.
Outside, in December, the air drives
little shudders into
the storm windows and I
lift up out of my chair, leaving
my place to my brother. I see
the family limned, an untidy
crosshatching of small, terrible fates and
too meager buckings against history's
mesh—the plug-ugly, the Wanamaker,
the drunk, the never wooed.

A scythe of sectile
Retelling.

An axhead
Hones the stump of truth like
Nerve ends spuriously

Cat-o'-nine-tailing
A horse—

Anything so volatile—
Over and over
Imagination's brink.

We relish the infinite
And pin it like a butterfly
To a stretch board

Of mnemonics.
Balsa wood works well or
White pine.
For cooking outdoors—
Use oak.

This is where science
Metes out credence.
Heat not languor
Razes valence:
Violence we can measure.

Better to boil bad water and
Learn to cow ourselves
Into ability.

Huge white Conestogas
Drift in and out
Of our conjunctival vision

So we work for a living
Stay drunk with
The fruit of
Two hundred years of national pride:

Lost destiny—
A continent slowly leaking into the swell. . .

The only nation I ever loved is divine &
ragtag like a second-string team. . .
The baseball flies over the railroad tracks

just missing a locomotive loaded with heifers.
We say *texture like leather* but we mean *something
akin to autonomy is dying*. A rain falls

over our towns and fields. A run is barely batted in.
Geese overhead undo in a shaggy & vacant breeze all
we have ever done. We have done

nothing & migratory leadership is a process we
recognize: the poke in, the ease out.
We are replaced by our own sex & nearly

perish in the untaking. Our nerves grow mean &
sullen & we roll and pitch a yawing bravado
when we least need it so

we stomach what we can stomach &
our stomachs growl menacingly wishing to
"lie down in darkness" with truly stoic food.

We eat greens. The clouds goose-step across the sky
like men uneasy, alert with uneasiness. We say
what isn't sold is remaindered & we aren't and we are.

We conclude exhortingly specific with shouts, with
language, with our pennants flying for the home
team,
with horns honking, with hormonal imbalance,

with feelings distinct that—discussing our good
deeds, municipal & partial, with the friendly
ornithologist, scanning the honkers wisping

off south—they are not the right ones to come out
with.

Today I sat on the dock in the sun
raking the last coals of
my body into the inlet.
Fear won't sizzle, won't
give up enough of its steam
to shape into a horse
to spur over the rooftops.
Sometimes I settle into a contented
disobedience like
a clanging ringer of a thrown
horseshoe. I won't leave here,
I won't stop this
revisionist version of my
neverending loop of nostalgia.
The milk on the porches
in a small town is cold,
a vireo sits eyeing
the shiny caps.
Nesting is a territorial activity,
the whole landscape
suddenly coming into focus!
It's here without my knowing it,
the pull of witch hazel
divining water—
the need to sleep.

Idleness isn't so dispiriting—I keep
having solid weeks of it. I sit and smoke
like a jerk and secretly mimic the herky-jerkiness

of TV static. Sometimes a friend
comes by saying something like "Epilogues
are romantic disengagements. . ." and

it's like discovering during recess
that you had grabbed your sister's lunchbag
by mistake. Liverwurst, ick! So I am

excused for the day & am pleased to
find a walk through a brown weedy field so adequate.
Now I am sitting so still the moon

drifting like a manatee over the Gulf Stream
is starting to pull my body's liquids
and with one spectacular little tidal wave

of my left hand I'm suddenly not here but
there, bending the marsh grasses of an estuary
with alarming velocity and limpidity,

talking with a girl late into the night, or
just now, back in my body,
grinning dumbly, drumming my fingers,

idle like the ocean's regal & perpetual motion.

Impenetrable, like spoilage, a few
sample days pooled
for the revival: a grand
wallop queued for a clout. Monday.
An oniony odor filling
the available air by molecular
collision, a grinding dispersal.
Tuesday. Several varieties of squash
limp in the sink, blanched
white, looking foreign, looking
domesticized... Wednesday. You wait
harnassing the room's
pallor as dusk steals it
and night in its turn.
You wait in the comfortable dark
thinking what mules can do—picking
a clever way over rubble,
pleasantly shy with soft
elliptical sneers. A doorknob
captures a half-disc of
specious light and returns it:
fierce glint of a grommet. Friday
and you wait. You will have
yesterday, the hug in the rain.
Come here, dear Saturday. A new penny
going dull in the folds
of a coat pocket.
                    The matinee—
cowboy movie, Appaloosa, semaphore, rose.
        Sunday, my rib-tickler. Death
will be a prompting—the right word
mouthed by a mouth.
                    You will leave intact.

Seeing, through the weave of the
woven curtains, daylight coming like
a lately gorgeous lover, I

admit morning like a butler fearing
the valuableness of someone else's fortune
in old Chinese bric-a-brac.

Vainglorious, I determinedly slight
all my little histories.
Morning nods, quiet & lambent like a sequin.

What am I dreading so?
The sun shifts its weight, towels
itself off, but was it raining?

In this light the horizons
balance perfectly. It's splendid &
I walk out the door.

I think *Time never accumulates: what
a small injustice!*
"Hello Morning," I call out, sweat now

covering me like furze. Morning is
sleepily shy, frail, failing
by the light getting ever stronger.

Together we die happily
on the porch, succinct, specular, speculating.

In the medieval histories we often
find shy, goatlike men counting
spansules or weighing powders, oblivious
of the millenarians cavorting
over the countryside,
rough-housing with wolves
in broad daylight. The Dark Ages—
everything misnomered! The Florentine
flask, discovered accidentally and discarded
by a glassblower in Trieste.
What amazing utility
found in the found, the unprepossessed!
A simpleton is awestruck by sunlight
focused by water standing
in a bottle and thrown magnificently
in a fulvous, circular spot, the size of
the head of a pin, on a map, generously
malformed, of what becomes
northern Italy. A fuliginous
odor and Milan burns. . .*Who the warring
angels?* and *how many?* What is asked
nudges and our hands, restless
like a fuller's, lay cloth straight
in folds, tending
the coarse fibers with a teasel's
neat grinning barbs. Or we close the book,
open another. Now the Renaissance
is declining, terrestrial attentions
turn celestial, Galileo quits teaching
fortifications and dedicates
Jupiter's newly-observed moons
to the house of Medici.

Inking and oiling the Heidelberg today, I
noticed the amber oil going
deep blue, mysterious, rampant, where
it dripped against the black finish. *Who
were the alchemists?* so never
disheartened, never formula-ed
enough to balk death. The notebooks
countenance little:
Metal remains metal.
Metal remains mostly metal.
History is the main thing:
mild effluvium, template
against the onslaught of darkness.
All bodies spin through it—
victim, virtuoso, life-giver...

Supper of leftover rice, oyster
soup and raw cabbage.
Two saucepans dirtied and cleaned. I like
a meal without preamble or interlude.
Nourishment's hail-fellow grip.
A commingling, metabolic,
non-cranial.
                    Dark January. A red mite
suspended in a glass of water.
A green towel draping lightly
over the back of a chair.
Swift white regrets.
                    One more romance, what
the malingerer dreams waking. . .midsummer,
following the boat trailer ruts
down to the lake, parting the grass
to follow the slow, stuttering,
nearly vertical flight of the spring azure.
She squeezed my hand, a breeze
rinsed us like a fable, like a squall.
                                    In Morse code
the letter V is *dot dot dot dash*. Like
Beethoven! like the fifth
symphony! cheerless trudging
grandeur recurring with a casual
force, a swimmer's stroke, aristocratic
like the letter V, or mnemonic,
the Roman way of writing the number 5
                                    My cognac —
strong and oil-colored. I read
a mystery: *In the next room, water*

running . . . Who drew the bath? The sleuths
Peered over the overturned rowboat . . .
there, the high rock walls of
Death Cove!

　　　　My abandonment— the glum
thoughts that first perceived me. My heart
fingered like a finger puppet, the remarkable
scale of what's me and what's *hors de moi*
brutally gonged, tympanum, frog's ear,
simulacrum . . .

　　　　　　The future in my hands.
The future open, cradled, awkward like a psalter.
The future greedy, the fickle future.

> *Not how one soul comes close to another but how it
> moves away shows me their kinship and how much
> they belong together.*
> —Friedrich Nietzsche

1

Dilute o gadzooksly dilute & suggesting
A sublime reprisal, the galaxies
Demand denial.
OK my little ones I cry
I will coerce you with a sigh. . .
How about this: this wilderness is nothing like
The *bildungsroman*, the rhomboid,
The dolloping squeeze of
The centuries!
It's the story of "what is left" & if
The "human element" tempers it,
It is only with a scoff.
A cynic's understanding is never an honest
Understanding but what I know
Is the stars hanging one night like
Pustules of grief over Ann Arbor.

2

One theory is this: intimacy is
Preeminently hazardous. Tonight I am
Full of the "me"
Being preposterous for
What is inconsolably aching now out of
A pleasantly blue & soothingly xerox

Beginning: I admit it: you were
So like everybody else & everybody else
Is this sad & this
Sleepless tonight.

It's October, huh?
How contend with the burlesque sorrow
The heart's slippage
The scree of my lost days. . .
It's not April & always abhorred &
My desire is to imbue the causality of seasons
With a sober touch like "Leaves,
I know how you work, so stop it!"

Or "Memory, you slow countersurge, sleep
This night with desire, it's
Just one more obligato gigolo."
I think of being placidly
Lake Placid & hunky dory or sailing
Down the Hudson with a trolling spoon or
A Turkish loo, sure, smooth, gleaming
Not unlike a quarterhorse.

I remember
A lorry driver with a penchant
For leaning out
The cab bellowing assurances to Welsh mountains:
— *Fucking aye, mate, fucking bloody aye. . .*
Ah the welter of tongues!
The names of places!
I wish I had a dossier on that!

3

Suppose I am a man, suppose
There's something intentionally vague
About the clouds
Tonight, no, suppose
Yesterday the tail end of a cold front
Left miniscule lavender clouds behind it
Like car exhaust, split ochre light.
Ravenous for some bigger squalor, I coaxed myself
Home, rich with glee.
Sitting in my chair, soundlessly alive & resisting
Delight, feeling like "the
Yellow thumping thing," I went & I go
"Gleep gleepgleep" in the conglomerate goo.

I let loose a handful of flies.
This isn't fun.
This is the jealous husband
Pawing cold books, sleepless all
Night, with too familiar hands.
The air is spiritual ha ha & blackly abundant
Ha ha & over & over again he pulls
The same clink, this cloud the size
Of a half dollar,
Out of the empty
Air into the empty bucket. It's standard,
Mean & it could be money. It's not.

The clouds swarm over &
Over a pallid sky, I kick the dog, I am
Reasonably spectacular,
I am like a butterfly,
I am in Mexico, I am
In a small & pleasurable conspiracy with
Three lesbians playing pool.

4

It's not the old maxim of sobbing "me,
I felt sorry for the picnickers:
They got so soaking wet!"
It's more like "I hitched your chastity belt
To a wavering star &
Stumbled mediocrely to a mediocre bar. . ."
Or "This love is like a rowboat
Being sculled,
One oar having disappeared
Overboard
In night fog."

So I promise
I wedge
Into your life like sorrow, like
Bother, like contrariness,
Like continue, like the here & now.
I can think of nothing
So tumultuously *ipso facto*:
My name is what my name is. . .

5

My mouth o my mouth!
To speak is to assassinate: the "moot shoot."
This is why the vowels
Traumatize in chorus
Like a monkey in a truss. It
"Could be wuss" & it is.
There's Our Saviour, natch, there's
The snares of sobriety,
There's beer beer beer
For the bleary aloof & there's
The morning "the next morning"
My mouth opens &

Like cotton
A tongue snakes out saying "Yowl,
I feel like a towel!"
There is no single thread to cling to. . .

6

Angry & awry, I love you violently, I think of
"Soft violence" & "artist & society" &
"This light so sporadic
I can't do any more for. . . for what?"
My old perseverence throbs bleak & constant:
There is a rock big enough for
A rock
In the Big River. This
Is fictitious & poignant, it is
Slowly particle-izing, it is invisible.

Oh hell, destiny isn't like this!
Let's have the disclaimers
Come before the rejoinders this time!
Why shouldn't this be Paris?
I think a hardon is
Something to be proud of & suddenly
A tidal wave fills Trouble Canyon!

No no no I think of something big & mediocre
Like the hat I wear playing poker.
The clock kicks the "real" air,
Hums "timelessly."

Here's a chummy little story: "In New York City,
I sit between a blonde waitress
And a tugboat *aficionado*. Gertrude Stein
Isn't a witticism away, but
She's knitting. Coming into the zoom

Of a lens, I feel like Dag Hammarskjold Plaza
Under six feet of rubbish.
A monorail wheezes by,
I light a cigarette &
Unravel peculiar pains. I think
Something's cuckolding this poem &
Revel in self-ambush. . ."

O the fierce motley of no delight!
O my remorse! O no remorse! O!

7

O unity! Unity in antiquity unity in "the corpse"
unity in copy-catting unity in ibis-like pensivity unity
in wood in taxis unity in farflung & jubilant vowel
sounds in rock & roll in drinking in the pishtushly
querulous phoneme in the paleontological study of the
mastodon in Tanzania in zany plains in Athens in
Delos lizards in Cycladean votives in ontogeny
recapitulating phylogeny in plankton in the ephemeral
sifted out of the intellectual like the last detail riding
out across the plains of unity in the roar of remedy in
regret in dispensing with destiny in the thickish bags
of premonition in the stirring of the commonplace in
the steel sudden blue of what our irony clothes in the
eternal suppliance of wonder in the acid-like & arcane
in distinct zoologic zones unity in the often-noted in
the snapped-out-of-sync in the ruse in the chiding
light in strife in the miles of history in alchemy in
the tangent missing the circle in hope & more in the

"immortal" tansy flowering with unseen whim in
the blown fuse of what's uncommanding & stark
                    unity in the funny
trooping of the star charts unity in the whorl &
point unity in refuge in the romantic standing-by
of days in the stark beach in the rowboat in bio-
thermal feedback in the others placing first second
& third in dear dead Nature's notebook. . .

8

The tomfoolery of
My drunken philanthropy isn't "Please be
My unity with impunity" but "If I had a nickel
For every woman
I ever loved & lost. . ."

There's something behind us now
Shimmering with a static quickness
Like faulty neon & I shiver
Into nay-saying.
Never again the marquee for sentiment, never
Again our movie, notoriously public &
Reeling itself
Out in an empty theater.
There's no dressing for sorrow,
My little Sputnik, but
Our one heart
Drifting over a sleepy town like
A flaming dirigible will suddenly
Coalesce & tether & sulk
Like a horse
On a hitching post. Should I come out
Shooting & leave

The saloon doors
Swinging alternately like catcalls? No no,
My little criminal, I should stay home & watch
The ever-burdening sunset but I rise
From the brow of some
Insanely preempting hill
To fire a slow round
Into the dumb bunches of buffalo
Snorting below.

9

Still night, still I walk this panic out
Down a dry sluice gate
Testing
The timbre of rock
Against rock. Over my shoulder the moon still
Hesitates to plunder, owl-like & swift
In flapping the air's warm ruffle.
O glint unstintingly, my flintlock!
O sweat out, my sweet rhapsody!
The planets shag about up there & we
Down here look monkishly about

Likening this bowl of light to
This hand "hoveringly tensile & adrift" cupping this
                                        water to

Water a pungency of geraniums. Ah! to
Flinch to beauty! Her red sprightly sails! To
Sail or to moor with gusto to
A dock of slight & wooden being is to
Quiet the quick skip of the heart's drive to
Sluff off what it cannot hold to. . .

10

There's the aphorisms
Settling out of this splendid knockabout

Gale wind, like leaves, surly,
Smiling miles off.

One is "The cricket is
A device the offended man, in retaliation,
Slips inside a letter to the
Offender. It erupts
The moment the envelope is opened."

One is "The revolution is
Never perpetual, running on its own feet.
The revolution is one foot stepping out unceasingly
Followed by
That same foot."

One is "Heating an empty pint
Of scotch
Condenses out one more pure
Half tablespoon
Of alcohol. It is so good
Some call it *the tic-toc of havoc*."

11

Uneasy with the pure shudder of the absolute,
I go warring hard alee & empty-handed & empty-
                                        handed,
I curl down to sleep
Like a dog.
Dreaming of the clouds! the clouds!

What cumbersome revelry! All of them
Leapfrogging about in puffy leotards, slapping
Each other's behinds with
Autochthonous burps.
How loathsome & fleecy & menial!

I shout beleagueredly "How about
A little homogeneity up there!"
I'm no handsome purist, but tying
This cloud like a jocular pariah
To my doorknob:

Certainly a big goof.
My simple contrivance of
Winsome companionship, love!
Lost like suicide denial, familial grief.
A mimic stopping *de rigueur*
By himself.

12

O Europe, sting of the dull sad Atlantic!
In Tuscany, the cypress like dark fangs, in Greece,
Poppies blaring like horns on the roadsides &
Lemons orbing like constellations in the orchard fog.
In Paris, speaking French,
Hampering the pure vowel with a dipthongal sigh,
                                        my longing
To earn a place among the "ranks of men" seemed
Retchingly earnest in a tawdry
Sort of way.

O seminal voracity of "what is bound to come!"
O flob off quick leak, you no gesture jinx!
Be intransigent like the weathervane but know this:
What I have learned is consoling,
Bookishly convenient &
Wondrous: "The isosceles triangle sits
Equally on two of its
Sides..." no no how about "The scalene
Triangle is equilaterally

Diathetic & contrary like
This is the perfect love or
This isn't the perfect love or
This isn't the imperfect love."

13

What sort of dog's parable now?

Romance is slow & a scrutinizingly
Abrupt lack of viability
Sometimes dogs it but

The girls & boys
Bike home together! Sometimes
Holding hands.
Watch out, smarty dogs!

14

O my mock comedy, my dimple, my kneecap!
My comeuppance gets the upper hand &
I delete myself with an enviable show
Of recourse. It's the old
"Zilch, cutie" brand
Of my gleeping, my "high command."
It's for crooning
"Ah know ah know ah know ah—" & it
Standardizes this love affair like the thud
Shut of a Webster's.

It's like being stopped rhetorically
By a blink: I land in the clink: I pull
A coin out of my earmuff:
I torque my little sentinel out of there
Like a beagle slipping on ice...

I am coiling with love...

15

The weather shifts its feet, mutters
Like a pigeon &
Ponders the befittingly amusing tyranny of
The unkempt seasons:
The relief of
Old tracks covered by
New snow, the lack of shelter, the
Perpetual dismay, the tirade I seek & forswear.

O my gray fleeting anesthesia, my
Cold standing distress, my smoke, my air!
I could hose the glow of this
Burning house all night &
In the morning
Only the spider's egg sack
Stuck to a shingle &
Four hundred baby arachnids blowing on sticky tethers
Like the names I call, like ashes
Stirred by morning's
Common wind

O my ruthlessness, my soothing...
All talk of love
Triggers something
Indefinably hungry & moribund
In me. I don't stop being
An inspecific humanoid but
I get ornery, I whet & hone my desire clean.

16

Down by the barn and sheds, where
The dog compasses a circle of bare earth
Around the stake, my father's

Second father, humpbacked, asthmatic, pumps
Water for the one calf.
Come winter, he'll butcher it &
I will stoop with him into this terrible innocence

Like an Indian boy in chino
Trousers—first blood, first lick of firewater.

The night being silent &
My ardor slowing to a slur,
I return to the sumptuous:
The tip of asparagus
Toiling the green breeze, the saturate
Fondling of the fondly motile air.

No more snuffing the quiet light
Of vision, no more
The remorseless straining,
The cohesive blot of self versus self.
I am right here & right here
I unstomach myself like a Japanese
Soldier captured after twenty years of fighting
The island spooks.
I return to the gadzooks of thinking &
My love jerks & smoulders
Like a Turk

Giving hosanna to the one city that can
Muscle him up, shove him under.

What I know is this:
Somewhere & scandalously my heartbeat will
Meet tempo with & temporarily
Demolish you, my cadence, my conductress, my cruel.

ERRATUM

P. 64, l. 24: for *old* read *dead*.